VideoWorkshop

for

Educational Psychology
Student Learning Guide with CD-ROM

Diana Murphy

Susan Daniels
California State University

Boston   New York   San Francisco
Mexico City   Montreal   Toronto   London   Madrid   Munich   Paris
Hong Kong   Singapore   Tokyo   Cape Town   Sydney

Preface

This student guide accompanies the *Allyn & Bacon Video Workshop for Educational Psychology*. It is designed to enhance your experience with the videos.

Each module includes
- **Learning Objectives** to help you focus your learning.
- **Observation Questions** that focus on the video itself.
- **Next Step** questions that ask you to go beyond the video by answering questions or completing projects.
- **Connecting to the Web** websites for further study.

Use this grid to correlate the modules in *Video Workshop for Educational Psychology* to your Allyn & Bacon textbook.

	Slavin *Educational Psychology*, 7/e	Woolfolk *Educational Psychology*, 9/e	Sternberg, Williams *Educational Psychology*
Personal, Gender, Social and Moral Development	Chapter 3	Chapter 3	Chapter 3
Individual Differences	Chapter 9	Chapter 4	Chapter 4
Exceptional Children	Chapter 12	Chapter 4	Chapter 5
Socioeconomic Status, Ethnicity, Gender and Language	Chapter 4	Chapter 5	Chapter 6
Approaches to Learning	Chapter 5, 6	Chapter 6, 7, 8, 9, 13	Chapter 7, 8
Motivating Students	Chapter 10	Chapter 10	Chapter 10
Classroom Management	Chapter 11	Chapter 12	Chapter 11
Assessment	Chapter 13, 14	Chapter 14, 15	Chapter 13, 14
Technology	throughout	throughout	throughout

Table of Contents

Module 1: Personal, Social and Moral Development

Learning Objectives:

After completing this module, you will be able to
1. explain the relationship between self-concept and academic achievement and what teachers can do to influence each.

2. identify effective strategies for teaching students the skills of negotiation and conflict resolution.

 *Video Clip 1: Teaching Respect*

Observation Questions:

1. How does this teacher educate her students about respect?

_____

_____

_____

_____

_____

_____

_____

Next Step:

1. Identify and give examples of at least three specific teaching practices in the primary grades that you believe threaten self-esteem.

   _____

   _____

   _____

   _____

   _____

   _____

2. In pairs or small groups, brainstorm developmentally appropriate activities that can be incorporated in the regular classroom to provide students with the opportunity to practice sharing and respectful behaviors. Share your ideas with the class.

   _____

   _____

   _____

   _____

   _____

   _____

3. Visit the website for "Current Trends in Character Education
(http://www.teach-nology.com/currenttrends/character_education/)."
Read about one of the programs listed here, then summarize and critique
it. Do you think it would work with at-risk children? Children from many
varied cultures? How would you change it to meet the needs of various
populations?

_____

_____

_____

_____

_____

_____

_____

_____

_____

_____

_____

_____

_____

_____

_____

 *Video Clip 2: Social Skills Development*

Observation Questions:

1. How does using a conflict resolution team teach children appropriate positive social skills?

_____

_____

_____

_____

_____

2. Do you believe this method of dealing with conflict would be effective in all circumstances? Explain.

_____

_____

_____

_____

_____

_____

_____

Next Step:

1. In a small group, plan and perform a role-play scenario that could be recreated in the classroom for use with elementary, middle-school or high school students, and that would give the students the opportunity to try-out positive approaches of negotiation and conflict resolution. Choose a grade level and a topic or situation appropriate for that grade level. Outline your plan here.

_____

_____

_____

_____

_____

_____

_____

_____

_____

_____

_____

_____

2. One criticism of home schooling is the concern that children will not learn the necessary social skills to function later in life. Do you agree with this? Support your answer. You may want to visit websites about home schooling for information. Begin with the About.com site: Homeschooling in the USA: http://homeschooling.about.com/library/weekly/aa072999.htm.

_____

_____

_____

_____

_____

_____

_____

_____

MODULE ONE Connecting to the Web:

Current Trends in Character Education: these are websites for teaching character education at the elementary level. http://www.teach-nology.com/currenttrends/character_education/

About.com site: Homeschooling in the USA
http://homeschooling.about.com/library/weekly/aa072999.htm

Teaching Academic and Social Skills to Students in Small Groups: Introductory page to cooperative learning, an approach to teaching students in small groups to improve academic achievement, social skills, and language development. Compiled by the California Department of Education.
http://www.cde.ca.gov/iasa/cooplrng.html

A Conflict Resolution Protocol for Elementary Classrooms
http://www.responsiveclassroom.org/feature_10.htm

Module 2: Individual Differences

Learning Objectives:

After completing this module, you will be able to
1. define multiple intelligences.

2. describe ways of applying multiple intelligence theory to differentiate instruction to meet the need of diverse learners.

 *Video Clip 3: Multiple Intelligences in the Classroom*

Observation Question:

1. Outline how these teachers demonstrate Gardner's Theory of Multiple Intelligences in this clip. Be sure to list each element they employed, and the purpose of each element.

_____

_____

_____

_____

_____

_____

_____

_____

_____

_____

_____

_____

Next Step:

1. Write a paragraph describing one of your best learning experiences, in or out of school. Discuss which intelligences were most fully engaged during this experience.

_____

_____

_____

_____

_____

_____

_____

_____

_____

2. Describe which of Gardner's eight intelligences you feel to be your strongest and which are your least fully developed. How do you feel that this profile or pattern of multiple intelligences may influence your teaching and work with students?

_____

_____

_____

_____

_____

_____

3. Gardner says that barring brain damage or other serious injury, everyone is capable of developing abilities in each of the intelligences or at least to a moderate capacity. Describe a personal development plan (activities and experiences you could cultivate in your life) that would help you extend your abilities in the area of your least developed intelligence.

_____

_____

_____

_____

_____

_____

4. Here are brief descriptions of three simple, traditional primary lessons in school. Select one and transform it so that it addresses at least four of Gardner's multiple intelligences (linguistic, logico-mathematical, spatial, bodily-kinesthetic, musical, interpersonal, intrapersonal, and naturalist). Use a separate sheet of paper for your answer.

Lesson 1:
A third-grade teacher has children read a section of a story about a child who lives on a farm. In this section, fall and harvest are described. After the children have read the story, the teacher asks basic comprehension questions: What did the boy do when his father scolded him for playing and not working? How did he feel? What did he do next?

Lesson 2:
At their seats, children complete a worksheet that contains math addition problems. Children are just learning about place value and are solving problems with answers greater than 10. As the children work, the teacher calls small groups up to meet with her. She goes over how carrying is used.

Lesson 3:
At their seats, children read a chapter about field birds in their science book. It presents photographs and information on birds of different kinds – chickadees, nut-hatches, and so on. When children have finished, they answer questions at the end of the chapter. They then bring their papers up to the teacher to be corrected.

MODULE TWO Connecting to the Web:

Gardner's Theory of Multiple Intelligences
http://www.newhorizons.org/trm_gardner.html

How Technology Enhances Howard Gardner's Eight Intelligences
http://www.america-tomorrow.com/ati/nhl80402.htm

Charles Edward Spearman (1863-1945) – developed a theory of general intelligence long before Gardner.
http://www.psych.su.oz.au/difference5/scholars/spearman.html

The International Society for the Study of Individual Differences foster research on temperament, intelligence, attitudes and abilities.
http://www.issid.org/issid.html

Module 3: Exceptional Children

Learning Objectives:

After completing this module, you will be able to

1. explain the role of classroom teachers in working with students with exceptionalities.

2. explain how different exceptionalities – mental retardation, learning disabilities, communication disorders, visual and hearing impairments – affect student learning.

3. explain how instructional strategies can be adapted to meet the needs of students with exceptionalities.

 *Video Clip 4: Adaptations in the Inclusive Classroom*

Observation Question:

1. What adaptations did you observe in these classrooms? What was the purpose of each modification?

_____

_____

_____

_____

_____

_____

_____

Next Step:

1. Visit a regular education classroom that includes special needs children, and note how the teacher incorporates both the special needs and general education children's abilities into the lesson plan. What special adaptations are made to accommodate disabilities?

_____

_____

_____

_____

_____

2. What concerns do you have about your own ability to teach students with special needs? Where or from whom do you think you might acquire information, resources, or support to help you grow in this area?

_____

_____

_____

_____

_____

_____

_____

_____

 *Video Clip 5: Lily*

Observation Question:

1. What tools does Lily use to enable her to communicate better? Look beyond the deficit aspect of special needs, and identify strengths you observed in Lily.

_____

_____

_____

_____

_____

_____

2. What purpose do peer tutors serve in the classroom?

_____

_____

_____

_____

_____

_____

_____

Next Step:

1. Work with a partner or in a small group to outline a plan for additional peer tutoring or individualized activities you feel would enrich and appropriately extend Lily's learning experiences.

_____

_____

_____

_____

_____

2. What are some reasons some individuals and groups have objected to establishing mainstreaming and inclusion programs in the public schools?

_____

_____

_____

_____

_____

_____

_____

3. What is your position on full-inclusion programs for students with disabilities? What might be some benefits for them and their general education classmates?

_____

_____

_____

_____

_____

_____

_____

MODULE THREE Connecting to the Web:

Find out more about inclusion at the website for the Council for Exceptional Children (CEC), http://www.cec.sped.org/.

The Inclusion Network - The Inclusion Network is a non-profit organization whose staff and volunteers partner to promote inclusion of people with disabilities in the Greater Cincinnati community.
http://www.inclusion.org/

American Disability Association
www.adanet.org/

Internet Resources for Special Children
www.irsc.org/

National Information Center for Children and Youth with Disabilities (NICHCY)
www.nichcy.org/

Office of Special Education Programs
www.ed.gov/offices/OSERS/OSEP/index.html

Module 4: Cultural and Language Differences

Learning Objectives:

After completing this module, you will be able to
1. explain the role that culture and language play in school success.

2. describe the ways that schools and classrooms can be adapted to meet the needs of multicultural students.

 *Video Clip 6: Teaching in Bilingual Classrooms*

Observation Questions:

1. Why is teaching children from diverse cultures a special challenge?

_____

_____

_____

_____

2. What techniques are demonstrated by the teachers in this clip to facilitate instruction?

_____

_____

_____

_____

Next Step:

1. The debate over the efficacy of bilingual instruction has gone on for years and will most likely continue in this country. Browse the Internet for articles on both sides of this subject, and write about your views. Prepare a brief presentation for your classmates.

_____

_____

_____

_____

_____

_____

_____

_____

_____

_____

_____

_____

MODULE FOUR Connecting to the Web:

National Association for Bilingual Education: National organization promotes the education of language-minority students. http://www.nabe.org/

National Association for Multicultural Education was founded in 1990 to support efforts in educational equity and social justice. http://www.nameorg.org/

Clearinghouse for Multicultural/Bilingual Education: http://www.weber.edu/mbe/htmls/mbe.html

Multicultural Pavilion provides resources for the classroom. http://curry.edschool.virginia.edu/go/multicultural/home.html

Multicultural Education Kiosk is intended as an introduction to multicultural education theory and practice, providing tools and online resources that promote social justice and equality. http://personal1.stthomas.edu/ARUNCHEY/index.htm

Module 5: Approaches to Learning

Learning Objectives:

After completing this module, you will be able to
1. discuss various memory aids students can use.

2. define experiential learning, and explain the benefits of learning with this technique.

 *Video Clip 7: Memory*

Observation Questions:

1. What is C.U.E., and how does it impact long-term memory?

_____

_____

_____

_____

_____

_____

_____

_____

_____

Next Step:

1. Conduct the following experiment with 2 students in your class. Present them with this list of shopping items and give them 30 seconds to study it. Ask one person to study the list and memorize it. Ask the other person to try organizing the material in a different way to help remember it. Who had more success? Why?

lettuce	butter	cereal	coffee	bologna
mayonnaise	eggs	soup	bacon	ketchup
chocolate chips	bread	laundry detergent		cream cheese
milk	hamburger	flour	bagels	cookies

_____

_____

_____

_____

_____

2. Acronyms and acrostics serve as useful memory aids for many people. The fictitious name "ROY G. BIV" is an example of an acronym used to remember the colors of the spectrum (Red, Orange, Yellow, Green, Blue, Indigo, Violet). "Every Good Boy Does Fine" is an example of an acrostic used as a memory device for remembering the lines on the treble cleft. In a small group, try to come up with a list of 8-10 more commonly used memory devices such as these.

_____

_____

_____

_____

_____

_____

_____

_____

_____

3. Write a paragraph regarding strategies you have effectively used for
    committing information to memory. Also address how you think you
    might be able to assist students in acquiring such strategies.

_____

_____

_____

_____

_____

_____

_____

_____

_____

_____

Video Clip 8: Experiential Learning

Observation Questions:

1. What are some ways experiential learning might be used?

_____

_____

_____

_____

_____

2. What is immersion, and why is it important in experiential learning?

_____

_____

_____

_____

_____

_____

Next Step:

1. Compare experiential learning to another learning process, such as project-based learning or simulations. What are the advantages and disadvantages of experiential learning over the others?

_____

_____

_____

_____

_____

2. Choose a topic that would best be taught using experiential learning, and create a lesson plan for it. Explain why this is the best method for learning this topic.

_____

_____

_____

_____

_____

_____

_____

_____

_____

_____

_____

_____

_____

_____

3. Recall a time that you were involved in an experiential learning activity, whether in school or out of school (scouts, camp, etc.), and write a descriptive paragraph. Include 3-5 reasons why this experience was meaningful or useful to you.

_____

_____

_____

_____

_____

_____

_____

_____

_____

4. Some teachers feel that experiential learning is a positive and profound approach and an excellent educational experience. Some teachers shy away from experiential learning because it is "too complex and difficult to organize." In a small group, construct a Force-Field Analysis chart (forces for/forces against) or a PMI (Plus, Minus, Interesting) chart to assess these aspects of the experiential learning approach.

Forces For	Forces Against

P	M	I

MODULE FIVE Connecting to the Web:

This site examines 12 different theories on how people learn: http://www.funderstanding.com/about_learning.cfm.

Theory Into Practice database has short articles about 50 major theories of learning and instruction. http://tip.psychology.org/

Sites related to learning and memory: http://www.supermemo.com/english/links.htm

Module 6: Motivating Students

Learning Objectives:

After completing this module, you will be able to
1. describe how classroom climate variables promote student motivation.

2. identify instructional factors that promote student motivation.

 *Video Clip 9: Motivation*

Observation Questions:

1. In this example, how does PBL motivate students to learn?

_____

_____

_____

_____

_____

_____

_____

_____

Next Step:

1. Why do you think choice and elements of control are essential components of human motivation?

   _____

   _____

   _____

   _____

   _____

2. Design a project for a sixth grade science class using project-based learning. Focus on ways to motivate students to learn as much as possible about the subject. What is the "hook"? What is the expected end result?

   _____

   _____

   _____

   _____

   _____

   _____

   _____

   _____

MODULE SIX Connecting to the Web:

Motivating Students to Learn - The conference on Hard Work and High Expectations brought together prominent researchers who addressed the topic of student motivation from different social, cultural, and instructional perspectives.
http://www.kidsource.com/kidsource/content3/work.expectations.k12.4.html

This list of helpful ideas for motivating students comes from the University of Oregon Teaching Effectiveness Program.
http://darkwing.uoregon.edu/~tep/tshooting/motivating.html

Motivating Students to do Quality Work, from Rethinking Schools Online.
http://www.rethinkingschools.org/Archives/12_03/motive.htm

Module 7: Classroom Management

Learning Objectives:

After completing this module, you will be able to
1. explain how instruction and classroom management contribute to productive learning environments.

2. identify essential teaching skills that help create productive learning environments.

3. explain the benefits of active learning approaches for minimizing classroom management issues.

 *Video Clip 10: Classroom Management*

Observation Questions:

1. Explain the relationship between classroom management and active learning.

_____

_____

_____

_____

_____

_____

_____

Next Step:

1. Interview two teachers, individually, about their classroom management procedures. Introduce yourself and inform the teachers that you are there to interview them specifically about their classroom management procedures, including the following:

    a. How are students to signal they want your attention or help?
    b. How do you call on students during whole-group activities?
    c. What are your guidelines and expectations for small-group, active learning projects? How do you respond if a student disregards your guidelines or rules?
    d. How are students to obtain materials for instructional activities?
    e. How are students to store and organize their materials?
    f. How and when are students to enter and exit the classroom?
    g. What are procedures for students going to the drinking fountain or bathroom?
    h. How do you set up expectations and manage noise level in the classroom, especially during group work time?
    i. Describe your expectations for classroom behavior and the consequences for misbehavior.

    Summarize the responses on a separate sheet of paper. Then respond to these questions as you think you would ideally wish to set up your own classroom.

2. Visit the website http://education.indiana.edu/cas/tt/v1i2/what.html and answer the questions to determine your classroom management profile. Were you surprised by your score? In which areas do you think you need to improve?

_____

_____

_____

_____

_____

_____

MODULE SEVEN Connecting to the Web:

"School Discipline" by Joan Gaustad. *ERIC Digest*, Number 78.
http://www.ed.gov/databases/ERIC_Digests/ed350727.html

Classroom Management: This is a list of links to classroom management sites:
http://jaring.nmhu.edu/classman.htm

Teachnet.Com - Classroom management techniques.
http://www.teachnet.com/how-to/manage/

Module 8: Assessment

Learning Objectives:

After completing this module, you will be able to
1. describe and explain basic assessment concepts.

2. explain the benefits and risks involved in using standardized testing to assess learning.

 *Video Clip 11: Standardized Tests*

Observation Questions:

1. What is norm-referenced measurement? When should it be used?

_____

_____

_____

_____

2. What is criterion-referenced measurement? When should it be used?

_____

_____

_____

_____

_____

_____

Next Step:

1. Do you believe the emphasis on standardized test taking and the resultant pressure it places on children and teachers helps or hinders genuine learning?

_____

_____

_____

_____

_____

2. Some educational professionals suggest that state and national curriculum and performance standards be established for all students to meet – not an easy matter, and one that can lead to criticism related to elitism, wrong approach or methodology for diverse populations, and possible disenfranchisement of students. Choose an area of critique, locate an article related to this concern, and bring the article and your review of this position to the next class session. Make a brief (3-4 minute) overview presentation of your selected issue for your classmates.

3. Visit the *American School Board Journal* website listed in the Connecting to the Web section below on "teaching to the test." What is your opinion of "curriculum alignment"? Is it synonymous with "teaching to the test," and if so, is it harmful to students?

_____

_____

_____

_____

_____

4. What do you feel is the most important function of evaluation: feedback, information or incentive? Explain.

MODULE EIGHT Connecting to the Web:

This site provides links to major stories on national education testing from *The Washington Post.*
http://www.washingtonpost.com/wp-srv/politics/special/testing/keystories.htm

A site developed by the editors of The American School Board Journal, this includes articles on the controversy over "teaching to the test" and other relevant topics.
http://www.asbj.com/achievement/aa/index.html

This is a listing of sites from the Michigan Electronic Library on alternative assessment.
http://mel.lib.mi.us/education/edu-assess.html

The National Center for Fair & Open Testing (FairTest) is a nonprofit advocacy organization dedicated to preventing the misuse of standardized tests.
http://www.fairtest.org/

ERIC: On Standardized Testing
http://ericeece.org/pubs/digests/1991/perron91.html

History of Standardized Testing
http://or.essortment.com/standardizedtes_riyw.htm

Module 9: Technology

Learning Objectives:

After completing this module, you will be able to
   1. discuss current trends and issues with respect to the use of information technology in teaching and learning.

 *Video Clip 12: Managing Technology in the Classroom*

Observation Questions:

   1. What advantages to using technology are demonstrated on this clip?

   _____

   _____

   _____

   _____

   2. How can technology be misused in schools?

   _____

   _____

   _____

   _____

   _____

   _____

3. What is an "acceptable use policy"? What should it include?

_____

_____

_____

_____

_____

_____

_____

_____

Next Step:

1. In 1922, Thomas Edison predicted that "the motion picture is destined to revolutionize our educational system and... in a few years it will supplant largely, if not entirely, the use of textbooks." In 1945, William Levenson of the Cleveland public schools' radio station claimed that "the time may come when a portable radio receiver will be as common in the classroom as is the blackboard." In the 1960s, B.F. Skinner believed that with the help of the new teaching machines and programmed instruction, students could learn twice as much in the same time and with the same effort as in a standard classroom.

    a. Did motion pictures, radio, programmed instruction, and television revolutionize education?
    b. Will computers become as much a part of the classroom as chalkboards?
    c. What do you predict the public school classroom of the year 2050 will be like?
    d. Will the role of the teacher be any different than today due to the use of technology?

_____

_____

2. Meet with a partner and discuss how you would respond to a parent who questions you about the benefit of using CD-ROM material in teaching. Summarize your answer here.

_____

_____

_____

_____

_____

_____

_____

_____

_____

Video Clip 13: Using Technology in the Classroom

Observation Questions:

1. What is an adaptive keyboard?

_____

_____

_____

_____

2. What kinds of students can benefit from this technology?

_____

_____

_____

_____

3. What are the advantages for a teacher who utilizes an adaptive keyboard with students?

_____

_____

_____

_____

_____

Next Step:

1. Write a lesson plan on a geography topic that involves the use of an adaptive keyboard for a physically handicapped student in a regular education classroom. You may choose to have an aide or a peer work one-on-one with the student. Include an element of the plan that requires parental involvement.

MODULE NINE Connecting to the Web:

Surfing the Net with Kids provides links to an amazing variety of topics for the entire school calendar and beyond: http://www.surfingthenetwithkids.com/

Virginia Department of Education Acceptable Use Policies: A Handbook. http://www.pen.k12.va.us/go/VDOE/Technology/AUP/home.shtml

Technology Integration in Education
http://www.pen.k12.va.us/go/VDOE/Technology/AUP/home.shtml

Assistive Technologies from the International Dyslexia Association
http://www.interdys.org/technolo.stm

NOTES

NOTES

NOTES

NOTES

NOTES

NOTES

NOTES

NOTES

NOTES

NOTES

NOTES

NOTES